Amsterdam Travel Guide

The Top 10 Highlights in Amsterdam

Table of Contents

Introduction 6

1. Grachtengordel 9

2. Rijksmuseum 13

3. Van Gogh Museum.....................................15

4. Bloemenmarkt..17

5. De Wallen..19

6. Koninklijk Paleis...23

7. Albert Cuypmarkt......................................26

8. Vondelpark..28

9. Leidseplein 31

10. Het Scheepvaartmuseum.......................34

Introduction

Amsterdam's greatest charm may also be its greatest mystery: how does such a historical city also serve as the most liberal metropolis in the world? From Van Gogh to the Red Light District, the Dutch capital city remains an intriguing mix of old and new.

One of the most popular travel destinations in Europe, Amsterdam is a compact and cosmopolitan city that invites exploration. Dubbed the "Venice of the North" due to its 100 plus canals, the capital of the Netherlands allows for enjoyable sight-seeing adventures on foot, bike or boat. Whichever way you decide to see it, you are bound to enjoy one of the world's most beautiful cities.

Attractions such as the wonderful 17th century city center give Amsterdam a face that is recognized the world over. A delightful way to experience the Dutch capital from a different angle is by taking a scenic canal cruise in the Grachtengordel, past the appealing and well-preserved Dutch Golden Age architecture that offers a quaint backdrop to the city.

Amsterdam also boasts a number of world-class museums. The Rijksmuseum houses the greatest collection of paintings from the Dutch Golden Age. Here you can feast your eyes on the world-famous "Night Watch" by

Rembrandt, among other masterpieces on display. Other Amsterdam museums not to miss are the Van Gogh museum and the Het Scheepvaartmuseum.

The Dutch capital is also famous for its Brown Cafes or pubs and "coffee shops" that sell cannabis. The best place to sample the Dutch "coffee" culture would be in and around the Leidseplein, the most popular square in Amsterdam. At this vibrant center, you can never get bored among the lively street performers, freestyle musicians, buskers, clowns, acrobats, break dancers and other entertainers.

Europe's largest outdoor market is also located in Amsterdam. The Albert Cuyp Market has been operational since the late 19th century and is today a tourist favorite that offers a fascinating glimpse into the lives of locals, including a pleasant introduction to Amsterdam's love of pancakes. At the colorful Bloemenmarkt floating flower market, you can discover the Dutch flower culture.

Amsterdam is not all concrete jungle as it does have its own green oasis in the center of the city. At Vondelpark, locals and tourists escape the city to gather for a relaxing atmosphere amid well-tended gardens. After a day of exploring, kick back and unwind on benches overlooking small ponds, flower gardens, walking and biking trails.

No visit to Amsterdam is complete without a tour of De Wallen, the Dutch capital's infamous Red Light District. A familiar haunt for pleasure seekers since the 14th century, De Wallen does offer more than just sex and alcohol. Beneath its promiscuous façade of sexy lingerie-clad girls behind red-lit windows are pretty canals, great bars and restaurants, as well as Oude Kerk, the oldest church in the Netherlands.

From the colorful flower markets, to fine art museums, from the red light district to the cannabis-selling "coffee shops", you are bound to find something unique and exciting to discover in Amsterdam at every turn. Amsterdam may very well have you planning your next visit, even before you leave.

1. Grachtengordel

When you think of Amsterdam, the first thing that comes to mind is canals galore. You do not need to seek out the canals of Amsterdam for they are everywhere. The heart of Amsterdam is divided by a neat series of over 165 canals that give definition to the Dutch capital. Built in the 17th century, the canals remain largely intact, providing a wonderfully unique backdrop to the city.

The Grachtengordel is the canal district in Amsterdam, characterized by the city's old center formed from concentric belts of canals in a network of streets, bridges, docks, houses and water side cafes. The 4 main canals are the Singel, Keizersgracht, Herengracht and Prisengracht.

The world famous canals of Amsterdam were built with the aim of controlling the flow of the Amstel River, as well as adding acres of dry land to the city. The wealthy merchants of Amsterdam soon realized that the canals were also ideal spots for showcasing their mansions.

Amsterdam's canals give the Dutch capital a feeling of space, peace and freedom, and transform it into one big open-air museum. The best way to experience the canals is on a boat cruise. You can rent your own boat and captain yourself, or go on a tourist cruise. Canal tour operators offer various cruises that range from hour-long excursions to candlelit cruises.

A good spot to begin your canal boat tour is with one of the many tour operators located at Damrak by the Central Station or Rokin by the Spui, as well as the area around the Leidseplein. The tour will take you around the city and through the harbor. A multi-lingual guide will introduce you to notable canal houses and old warehouses typical of the Dutch Golden Age.

A boat ride along one of the many canals in the city provides a relaxing way of viewing the traditional Dutch architecture. The canals are lined with lime and elm trees and crossed over by over a thousand bridges.

Certain parts of the old city center date from the 13th century and feature many impressive buildings that overlook the canal district. This is where the wealthy of the Dutch Golden Age lived. Here you can admire the beautiful traditional merchant houses, pretty bridges and thousands of houseboats.

As you work your way around the over 100 kilometers of canal, be sure to also view the dozens of islands, the 1,500 bridges and 1,550 monumental buildings. Also try to spot the older remnants of the original defensive canals, most of which were incorporated into later renovations, such as the Singel which began its life as a moat in the 1400s.

Look out for the Magere Brug, a traditional Dutch double-leaf draw-bridge that connects the sides of the Amstel River. The bridge master opens the bridge every 20 minutes to allow the boats to pass through the canal. The original bridge was constructed in 1670 and has not changed much since.

Another great way to explore Amsterdam's canal district is to travel as the Dutch locals do - on a bicycle. With an estimated 1 million bicycles circulating the city, Amsterdam is one of the bike capitals of the world. The flat and compact nature of the city makes cycling a fast and affordable way to travel in Amsterdam.

Visitors can also walk through the canal streets. You are bound to enjoy a stroll in this part of town which is typically very quiet as the small canal lanes are not suitable for motorized traffic. Take in a deep breath of fresh air brought in by the river, enjoy the magic of the canal district and experience Amsterdam's unique vibe.

Also stop at the Het Grachtenhuis or "Canal House Museum" where you can learn how the canals of Amsterdam were created. If you like boats, try to make it to Amsterdam in time for the various shipping and boating events held regularly in the city.

Another attraction within the central circle of land in Amsterdam's circular canal system is the Begijnhof, a narrow vaulted enclosed courtyard that originated as a 14th century residence for the sisterhood of Catholic Beguines.

Here, visitors can admire the Begijnhof Kapel, a charming structure fitted with stained-glass windows and marble columns. This is where the sisterhood worshipped in secret during the Reformation when their chapel was confiscated.

The lovely courtyard features a group of old houses that date from the 14th century built around a quiet charming garden. Here you will find the oldest wooden house in Amsterdam – the No. 34, which dates from 1465. The Begijnhof is today a religious center of silence. Visitors are welcome, but not in groups and talking should be done outside the gate.

2. Rijksmuseum

Rijksmuseum is the biggest and most important art and history museum in the Netherlands, which attracts over one million visitors every year. Occupying the northeastern section of Museumplein, it houses the greatest collection of Dutch art and history in the Netherlands.

The museum features a wonderful collection of 17th century Dutch Golden Age masterpieces. It is particularly famous for housing Rembrandt's 1642 painting *De Nachtwacht* or "The Night Watch". Fully named *Militia Company of District II under the Command of Captain Frans Banninck Cocq*, this painting is the ultimate crowd-puller which alone is worth the admission price.

Other celebrated works you can admire include *The Milkmaid* and *Woman Reading a letter* by Vermeer; van Ruisdael's *The Windmill at Wijk bij Duurstede*; and Jan Steen's *The Burgomaster of Delft and his Daughter*; among many others. The marvelous paintings housed in this museum are a reflection of the character and history of the Dutch people.

There are also unique sculptures and various antiquities present including traditional furniture, silverware, Delftware, doll houses and ship models. Its entire collection numbers over one million artifacts dating from the 13th century. Visitors can also admire the substantial collection of Asian art that is also found here.

For decades, the museum collection was housed in buildings all over the country until 1876 when construction of the Rijksmuseum started. The completed museum was opened in 1885 and currently has about 8,000 objects on display.

From 2003, the museum underwent a 10 year renovation and reopened in 2013. The renovation saw the previous classical and old fashioned atmosphere of the magnificent museum replaced by vast open expanses that make the exhibits more accessible and inviting. The stately dignified rooms of old were replaced by a new and unique way of grouping the works of the Old Masters.

Typically ranked in the top 20 museums of the world, the Rijksmuseum makes for a fascinating place to visit for the day. And as if the artworks aren't enough, be sure to take a look at the building interiors which are also very impressive.

3. Van Gogh Museum

Over 100 years after his death, Vincent Van Gogh is more popular than ever. Regarded as a trail blazer for contemporary art, Van Gogh was famous for his distinct style of sharp colors and rough lines. At the Van Gogh museum in Amsterdam, art lovers can learn the story of Van Gogh, the man, from childhood to his death at 37 years old.

Located on the northwestern side of Museumplein in Amsterdam, the Van Gogh museum is a modern museum housed in a 4-story building designed in the 1970s. On the top floor you can admire about 200 paintings from the Dutch Post-Impressionist era and 550 sketches that show Van Gogh in all his moods, which form the core of the collection.

This is the biggest Van Gogh collection in the world, and includes self-portraits, landscapes, stills including *The Potato Eaters*, and *The Yellow House*, which is also known as *The Street*. The collection is completed by hundreds of letters by the famous expressionist painter, many of his personal effects, as well as select works by his contemporaries and friends such as Gauguin, Monet and Daubigny.

On the second story, art lovers can have an intimate look at the evolving style of Van Gogh. On the third story you will find information on the troubled life of the artist, as well as the efforts that went into restoring his paintings.

Through his paintings, the museum chronicles Van Gogh's journey from the Netherlands where his work was somber and dark, and onto Paris where he discovered vivid color through the influence of the Impressionists.

The Van Gogh collection is often complemented by thematic expositions at the museum. To avoid the crowds, go late to the museum. On Friday nights, the museum opens till 10pm and offers a more relaxed and enjoyable environment.

4. Bloemenmarkt

Located between Koningsplein and Muntplein on the south bank of the Singel canal, the Bloemenmarkt is the world's only floating flower market. Every day of the week, flower vendors load floating barges and stands with all types of flowers and bulbs that the Netherlands is world famous for, in the process creating a wonderful place full of color.

Founded in 1862, the original market came about due to flower farmers who sailed the Amstel River to this spot to sell flowers from their boats. Today, the market features 15 different florists and garden shops, as well as souvenir stalls.

While locals shop here as well, the market is primarily aimed at tourists. The bulbs available for sale are designated as "ready for export", so visitors are able to buy daffodil, tulip, narcissus and other bulbs as a memento of their tour of the Dutch capital.

Visitors are certain to enjoy taking a walk on this street full of hundreds of different flowers in a multitude of colors. Stroll through the stunning array of bulbs, and delight in its explosion of color especially on a rainy day in Amsterdam. You can also buy cut flowers, seeds and garden supplies to take with you as a souvenir of your trip to the Netherlands.

True to Dutch culture, the stalls at Bloemenmarkt also sell cannabis starter kits, which contain a few cannabis seeds and some soil. It is legal to purchase marijuana seeds in Amsterdam.

5. De Wallen

De Wallen is the infamous Red Light District in Amsterdam, a designated area in the city where prostitution is legal. De Wallen is the biggest and best known of Amsterdam's red light districts and covers a number of canals and side streets to the south of the Central Station. It features an eclectic mix of brothels, adult shops, gay bars, live adult theaters, coffee shops and about 300 red light windows.

The most notable feature of De Wallen is the display of lingerie-clad girls who entice onlookers from behind windows illuminated by red lights. Hundreds of one-roomed apartments along the canals are rented by the sex workers. The rooms have windows large enough to allow prospective clients to literally "window shop" until they find someone of interest. Services start from 50€ and above.

There are also legal brothels within the district and in the surrounding areas known as privehuizen or "private houses". These are low-key brothels mainly located in residential neighborhoods that charge by the hour. Close by are also sex clubs associated with the Red Light District scene, where customers mix with each other and the girls in a bar setting. There are also live sex shows in some clubs.

No visit to Amsterdam is complete without paying a visit to its Red Light District. Located right in the middle of the city, where normal day to day life happens right next to prostitution, Holland's Red Light District is as much a Dutch symbol as cheese and clogs. While the red lighted windows are a more recent addition, prostitution in the De Wallen area has been ongoing for centuries.

Whether or not you wish to pay for the services on offer, an evening walk in the nightlife of Amsterdam's Red Light District is a recommended Dutch experience. There is a strong police presence to keep the neighborhood safe. And while visitors are welcome, taking photographs is not permitted.

There are always tourists present as well as local Amsterdammers. On weekends, the neighborhood features many traveling parties of men and women. The type of erotic entertainment on offer is particularly popular with groups of young European men on weekend bachelor parties.

The Netherlands legalized prostitution on the basis that you can never fully ban prostitution. Therefore it is best to allow it in the open, which makes it possible to control and regulate. Street prostitution however remains illegal in the Netherlands. Non-residents are not allowed to work in the sex trade as work permits are not issued for this work.

Ever since it was legalized in 2000, the Dutch sex trade has been the subject of intense fascination, risqué interest and in certain cases revulsion by those who may not have contemplated such a business before. Amsterdam's Red Light District is the main center of the legalized prostitution industry in the Netherlands.

While prostitution is legal in many European countries, nowhere in the world is it a major tourist attraction as it is in Amsterdam. Amsterdam's sex trade is a curiosity for some, and a reason to visit for others. While the offerings of the Red Light District are likely to put a blush on many cheeks, the locals of this liberal country are hardly fazed.

But there's much more to the Red Light District than just prostitution. There are numerous bars, restaurants, coffee shops and night clubs. Naturally this is the wild part of town, although there are also churches, a farmers' market and the homes of thousands of residents. You could also visit De Wallen during the day for some shopping, as well as to discover the interesting art and history of the area.

De Wallen is also the oldest section in Amsterdam and houses a number of historic buildings. One of its main attractions is the Oude Kerk, the oldest church in Amsterdam which has little houses clinging to its sides. The church building features an interesting octagonal bell tower designed in the Gothic Renaissance style and which was once used by sailors to find their bearings.

Built around 1250 AD, Oude Kerk is a big protestant church in which famous Amsterdammers were married or buried. Today, the church holds exhibitions such as the annual World Press Photo awards. A wonderful building in its own right, the church is open to the public in the afternoons.

6. Koninklijk Paleis

The Koninklijk Paleis is one of the royal palaces in the Netherlands which is located on the western side of Dam Square in the center of Amsterdam. With its façade of sandstone looming over the centrally located Dam Square, Koninklijk Paleis has been the firm favorite with tourists since it became state property in 1936.

This 17th century structure originated as the town hall, but was converted into a palace when Napoleon's brother was crowned King Louis I of Holland. Although Louis I did not enjoy the marble beauty of the building for long as he abdicated the throne in 1810.

The Koninklijk is an imposing Classical palace whose edifice and neoclassical façade betrays the ostentatious theme of the prestige and power that Amsterdam commanded in the 17th century. The palace's impressive dimensions, immense central hall and exquisitely carved statues are all reminiscent of Roman architecture.

Its Romanesque construction was fashioned around more than 13,500 wooden piles that were sunk into the ground. The building is also famous for its iconic statue of Atlas, the Greek titan, on the rooftop straining beneath the weight of the world that's on his back.

While its exterior was constructed in sandstone to mimic the public buildings of ancient Rome, the interior is a premier example of the elaborate Empire style of the early 1800s. The palace lives up to its reputation of opulence with glistening marble floors and lavish décor, which makes it a fascinating place to visit.

The breathtaking interiors are the main attraction in the palace, furnished with an amazing collection of antiques, and adorned with ornate carvings. Its walls are also adorned with superb art works, including the collection of the House of Orange-Nassau, and paintings inspired by Rembrandt.

Although still used for royal events by the Dutch Royal House, the palace is open to the public for most of the year. Visitors can explore the beautiful and elegant palace's magnificent interiors and discover the rich history of the building.

Visitors can take a peek at the vast bronze and marble carvings that adorn the Burgerzall, the Baroque "Citizen's Hall". A unique feature of the Burgerzall is the maps inlaid on the marble floors that depict Amsterdam as the center of the world.

Take a walk around the galleries, halls and rooms where you can admire the Empire collection, painted ceilings, chandeliers, early 19th century furniture and epic paintings and sculptures from the 17th and 18th centuries.

Today the palace also serves as a source of information on famous Dutch painters. Guided tours are offered by art historians and art-history students, although these must be scheduled 2 weeks in advance. If you prefer to go on a self-guided tour, there are mobile guides available for use.

7. Albert Cuypmarkt

Albert Cuypmarkt is the biggest day market in Europe. The busy market features more than 300 stalls lining almost a kilometer long street in the De Pijp area of Amsterdam. The stalls sell everything from fresh fruit and vegetables, flowers, leather goods, fish, spices, cheese, clothing, bedding and cosmetics.

Many of the stall-holders and residents of this neighborhood are from Morocco, Turkey and Suriname. The immigrant communities typically operate businesses aimed at their countrymen, thereby making De Pijp one of the more cosmopolitan areas in an otherwise homogenous city center. This mix of cultures gives the Albert Cuypmarkt a vibrant, multi-cultural feel.

The largest street market in the Netherlands, Albert Cuypmarkt was named after Albert Cuyp, a 17th century Dutch Golden Age painter. Situated within the Old South district of Amsterdam, the market has been operational since 1905. The market began as an assembly of street vendors and pushcarts, before growing so large as to force city authorities to formalize an official market in the area.

The market is today operational 6 days a week and offers groceries from all around the world. It also features vegetable stands, butchers and cheese sellers. This is where most locals do their shopping, although tourists can also enjoy visiting the market whether to shop or just stroll through and take in the atmosphere.

During your visit, be sure to sample the Dutch Stroopwaffels or "syrup waffles" which are a popular treat at the market. If you have a sweet tooth you will enjoy this delicate treat that comprises two fresh thin waffles enclosing a sweet caramel layer. Also try a plate of delicious Vlaamse frites or Amsterdam French fries.

8. Vondelpark

Originally named Nieuwe Park when it opened in 1865, Vondelpark is Amsterdam's central park. Located in the Oud-Zuid or "Old South" district of Amsterdam, to the west of Museumplein, Vondelpark is a popular gathering spot for both tourists and locals, with over 10 million visitors going there each year.

Inspired by the popular gardens of Victorian England, Vondelpark was originally built as a walking ground for the bourgeoisie, to walk and ride their horses, sit on the green lawns and drink in the tranquil beauty of its greenery. Located centrally, right in the middle of the city, the public park is 47 hectares in size, 8 of which is water.

The park also has an interesting history in that Amsterdam's council members were open to the possibility of lovers using the park for romantic trysts. The council sought to permit adults to have sexual intercourse in the park, as long as it was dark, and not near the playground areas, and as long as they "tidied up" after themselves. However, the Amsterdam police refused to allow this on the grounds that such activities were against the law.

The park got its present name in 1867 when a statue of Joost van den Vondel was erected inside the park. The statue of the famous Dutch 17th century playwright and poet became such a familiar landmark that park goers began calling the park "Vondelpark". The name change was formalized by city authorities in 1880.

Over the decades, the park has had a small stream and several paths alter formation, with some vanishing altogether. A sweetly scented rose garden continues to flourish, while a children's playground has been built. But even with all these changes, the park has remained a relaxing and beautiful green oasis, providing retreat from the concrete jungle of Amsterdam.

On sunny days, the park brims with life as people gather for picnics or to read a book. There are also skaters, joggers and a steady stream of entertainment from many performers, including fire-eaters and jugglers. You can also bike along the wonderful bike paths, or play soccer, badminton and Frisbee on the grass. At the park's south side, visitors can rent inline skates.

This English-style park has an abundance of lawns, ponds, thickets and winding footpaths where you can while away the hours. Go here to relax and unwind after a long day of exploring Amsterdam. Or just sit and admire the Picasso sculpture. The park also has several places to eat and drink where you can enjoy a herring sandwich and some Dutch beer.

If you're in Amsterdam between June and August, you can enjoy free plays, concerts and performances at the open-air theatre. Another lovely spot to enjoy at the park is the terrace of the Film Museum.

In 2010, the restoration of Vondelpark was completed after 10 years. Visitors can now enjoy the Blauwe Theehuis, a modernist pavilion dating from 1930. The pavilion, which was transformed into a café and restaurant with terrace, is worth paying a visit. Built in the New Functionalist style, this unique landmark looks like a giant blue straw hat.

9. Leidseplein

Every city worth its salt has a "happening" square and Amsterdam is no different. At the Leidseplein, you can take in the buzzing life of the Dutch capital in this relatively small square that more than makes up for its lack of grandeur with character and vibrance. This immense open square in the heart of central Amsterdam is without a doubt the thriving hub of the city.

Leidseplein is the entertainment section of Amsterdam. Lively eateries dot the square, as well as many cafes with terraces and restaurants, where visitors can sit back and enjoy the fun atmosphere of the square. There are also theatres, food vendors and markets selling produce, where locals come to shop or to see and be seen.

But the bustle doesn't end at dusk, for at night, Leidseplein transforms into a thriving club scene. For many locals, a night out in Amsterdam means a night on the Leidseplein. There's something for everyone, from pubs to trendy bars and dance clubs.

The liveliness of the square is best experienced during the evenings when street performers such as buskers, singers, dancers, clowns, acrobats, fire-eaters and family bands appear to entertain the crowds. Join in on the street performances if you dare.

During the summer, the Leidseplein teems with locals and tourists. During the winter months, a skating track circles the square and traffic is allowed to pass close to it, thereby making it easy to access at all times. Leidseplein is also very close to a number of other must-see Amsterdam attractions, which makes it the ideal spot to begin or end your day's exploration.

After a busy day of walking around Amsterdam, sit at one of the hundreds of old "Brown cafes" flanking the Leidseplein. You can enjoy a meal with local beer as you sit outside and watch the activities taking place on the square. Most Brown cafes offer a limited food menu of snacks, salads and sandwiches. Be sure to try out the local favorite bitterballen (fried balls of meat and potato).

Brown cafes are actually pubs that have an Old Dutch feel to them and a unique atmosphere due to the lively crowds of locals who patronize them. They are more like the extended living rooms of ordinary Amsterdammers. In fact, some of Amsterdam's renowned singers had their first teen performances in Brown cafés owned by their parents.

The cafes have a laid-back, casual feel, with a well-worn look, quirky decorations and old collectibles that often go with the name or theme of the café. Brown cafes are as much a part of the Amsterdam charm as the city's architecture and canals. Their name "Brown" derives from the thin dark wood walls and interiors stained by decades of cigarette smoke. Smoking is now banned in Dutch cafes.

Also at the Leidseplein, as well as at over 200 "coffee shops" in Amsterdam, you can buy small quantities of marijuana or hashish for personal use. This is yet another unique aspect of Amsterdam that makes it a popular world attraction. Such coffee shops also sell coffee and soft drinks but do not typically sell alcohol.

The reasoning behind the cannabis-selling coffee shops is the same as with the legalization of prostitution in the Netherlands: you can never fully ban all drug use, and therefore it is best to allow some of it in the open, which makes it possible to control and regulate. However, aside from hash and marijuana, other drugs remain fully banned in the Netherlands.

10. Het Scheepvaartmuseum

Het Scheepvaartmuseum is the National Maritime Museum of the Netherlands which is a captivating place to visit. A celebration of the Netherland's impressive naval history, the museum is a good place to enjoy artifacts from Amsterdam's rich nautical past. Here you can learn how sea trade made Amsterdam the wealthiest city in the world during the 1600s.

Het Scheepvaartmuseum is a modern museum housed inside a magnificent 17th century building, in which you can explore the world of ancient mariners. The former naval storehouse was constructed in 1656, and today houses the 18 rooms of artifacts and exhibits that make up the museum.

A visit to Het Scheepvaartmuseum is well worth it with its fascinating exhibits. Tourists can admire the numerous modern multimedia exhibits, a rich collection of fine paintings, remarkable ship models and old artfully-drawn maps.

Het Scheepvaartmuseum demonstrates how the Dutch dominated the seas with exhibits ranging from depictions of historical sea battles to 17th century weapons. The museum also has a collection of carvings to give you insights into how the sailors spent the time while at sea.

Also moored at its quay, the museum has a replica of the Amsterdam, an 18th century ship that sailed the route between the Netherlands and the East Indies, which visitors can explore. This enjoyable and colorful museum will help you understand the Netherlands' history as a small country that was one of the world's greatest sea powers just centuries ago.

Copyright © 2015. All rights reserved.

Except as permitted under the United States Copyright Act of 1976, reproduction or utilization of this work in any form or by any electronic, mechanical, or other means, now known or hereafter invented, including xerography, photocopying, and recording, and in any information storage and retrieval system, is forbidden without written permission.

The ideas, concepts, and opinions expressed in this book are intended to be used for educational and reference purposes only. Author and publisher claim no responsibility to any person or entity for any liability, loss, or damage caused or alleged to be caused directly or indirectly as a result of the use, application, or interpretation of the material in this book.

Printed in Great Britain
by Amazon